T0065331

Rooted and Built Up in Him

SHERRY J. MILLER

WESTBOW
PRESS®
A DIVISION OF THOMAS NELSON
& ZONDERVAN

WestBow Press books may be ordered through booksellers or by contacting:

WestBow Press
A Division of Thomas Nelson & Zondervan
1663 Liberty Drive
Bloomington, IN 47403
www.westbowpress.com
1 (866) 928-1240

ISBN: 978-1-5127-0360-3 (sc)
ISBN: 978-1-5127-0361-0 (e)

Library of Congress Control Number: 2015919168

Print information available on the last page.

WestBow Press rev. date: 01/07/2016

Contents

Foreword

I grew up in what many would consider a dysfunctional home. My father was an alcoholic, and my mother often worked two jobs. As a child I was subjected to sexual abuse repeatedly. By twenty-two I was the single mother of three and working hard to support my family.

At twenty-four I married. My husband, an alcoholic, was mentally, verbally, and physically abusive. As time went on, I became depressed and withdrawn and began to seek comfort in drugs. Life continued to spiral downward and I overdosed three times in an attempt to alleviate the emotional pain. I was finally committed to a mental hospital. After being released from the hospital, I was put into a Christian women's shelter where I met Sherry, the author of this book. She told me about God's love, forgiveness and salvation. Although I had grown up going to church, I had never had a personal relationship with Jesus Christ. I accepted Christ as my Lord and Savior and, with discipling, slowly began to grow as a Christian.

Today I live in freedom. I am free from drugs and from my bondage to sin. Though life is still hard, I have the peace and joy that comes from knowing Christ. God used this book to change my perspectives and mature me spiritually. I pray it will do the same for you.

Donna

Preface

In his book *Already Gone*, Ken Ham points out the tragic fact that two-thirds of the young people sitting in our churches today will eventually leave the church. We see young and old alike drifting away from their faith, like a ship drifting away from the harbor because it was not adequately moored. Of those drifting away, some were never true Christ-followers. The other drifters, though Christians, have not matured spiritually. As the busyness or trials of life increase, the people in this second group drift slowly away from their only source of true stability. Paul, concerned about the spiritual stability of the Colossian believers, writes, "As you therefore have received Christ Jesus the Lord, *so walk in Him, rooted and built up in Him and established in the faith,* as you have been taught, abounding in it with thanksgiving" (Col. 2:6-7, emphasis added).

As this passage points out, salvation is the first and foundational step to a life in Christ. But Paul goes on to command his readers to walk their talk. If you say you are a Christian, then walk just as Jesus walked. But this can only be done as we become deeply rooted in Christ through spiritual growth. A large, towering oak tree with a deep root system will be able to handle heavy rains and forceful winds. But the tree with shallow roots will quickly topple under the same conditions. As Christians, we live each day under the influence of the evil one with his value system and philosophies. Unless we are deeply rooted in God's Word and God's ways, we will be lured away— sometimes without even being aware of what is happening to us.

Those competing in the Olympic games have made it to the top because they spent years working hard with that goal in mind. As Christians, we too must have goals—spiritual goals. Many Christians wander aimlessly from day to day with no spiritual goals to keep them on track, so they see little to no spiritual growth. Like a tree with a shallow root system, the storms of life easily bring them down. This study starts with the foundation of salvation and then covers the many-faceted subject of spiritual growth. Spiritual growth requires effort. It requires setting goals. It requires commitment. This book will encourage you along that path.

I would love to be of help to you in any way that I can. Please feel free to contact me at <u>millersherryj@gmail.com</u>.

Acknowledgments

This book was a team effort to be sure. My loving and faithful husband has, throughout our marriage, made many sacrifices to allow me to do what God has called me to do. On this project, his editing skills were put to good use. Shelley Madson, my dear friend of nearly 30 years, has also been indispensable in her encouragement and friendship. She also spent many hours reading and suggesting improvements. Many thanks to both! My children, Caleb, Josiah, and Abigail, have been very patient and encouraging. I pray, my children, you will always focus on heavenly realities rather than earthly ones.

"As you therefore have received Christ Jesus the Lord, so walk in Him, rooted and built up in Him and established in the faith, as you have been taught, abounding in it with thanksgiving."

Colossians 2:6-7

1

Salvation

There are few certainties in life. But one certainty we all face is the certainty of death. The Bible tells us, "It is appointed for men to die once, but after this the judgment" (Heb. 9:27). This verse warns us that not only will each one of us die, but each of us will also stand before a holy Judge. God will judge us according to *His* righteous standard—not ours. We will either pass or fail. There is nothing in between. In Matthew 25, Jesus describes this time of judgment:

> "When the Son of Man comes in His glory, and all the holy angels with Him, then He will sit on the throne of His glory. All the nations will be gathered before Him, and He will separate them one from another, as a shepherd divides his sheep from the goats. And He will set the sheep on His right hand, but the goats on the left. Then the King will say to those on His right hand, 'Come, you blessed of My Father, inherit the kingdom prepared for you from the foundation of the world... and these [the people on His left, the "goats"] will go away into everlasting punishment, but the righteous into eternal life'" (Matt. 25:31–34, 46).

1. What two eternal destinies are described in these verses?

2. Each of us will spend eternity in one of these eternal destinies. "Have you come to a place in your spiritual life where you know for certain that if you were to die today you would go to heaven, or is that something you would say you're still working on?"[1]

3. "Suppose that you were to die today and stand before God and He were to say to you, 'Why should I let you into My heaven?' What would you say?"[2]

4. According to the following verse, of what can we be absolutely sure? "These things I have written to you... that you may know that you have eternal life" (1 John 5:13).

The overall theme of the Bible is how we, as humans, can gain eternal life. The purpose of this chapter is to examine what the Bible says about the subject of our eternal destiny and how we can be *sure* we are going to heaven when we die.

Read the following verses, and prayerfully consider what God is saying to you through His Word.

---

[1]   D. James Kennedy, *Evangelism Explosion* (Wheaton, IL: Tyndale House Publishers, Inc., 1996), 39.

[2]   Ibid., 40.

God Is Holy

Throughout the Bible we are told that God is holy. To be holy means to be separated from sin. In other words, God is morally perfect. As a perfect being, God cannot have an imperfect standard.

5. What does this verse say God requires of us? "Therefore you shall be perfect, just as your Father in heaven is perfect" (Matthew 5:48).

But perfection is a standard we cannot attain! Therefore, we will never deserve or earn a place in heaven by our own efforts. We, on our own, will always fall short of God's standard for heaven.

Our inability to earn or deserve heaven is because…

Man Is Sinful

The Bible tells us that we are the polar opposite of God. He is sinless; we are sinful.

- "For all have sinned and fall short of the glory of God" (Romans 3:23).
- "The heart is deceitful above all things, and desperately wicked; who can know it?" (Jeremiah 17:9).

Let's take a test to ascertain just how sinful we are:

- Have you ever disobeyed your parents?
- Have you ever told a little white lie or half-truth?

- Have you been jealous or envious for something you don't have?
- Have you ever used God's name lightly or in vain?

If we were honest with ourselves, we would admit to doing all of these. According to the Bible, then, we are disobedient, lying, covetous blasphemers! And we have examined only four of God's Ten Commandments (Ex. 20:1-17)![3]

6. How does the following verse describe our relationship with God before we were saved? "And you, who once were alienated and enemies in your mind by wicked works, yet now He has reconciled in the body of His flesh through death ..." (Colossians 1:21–22).

7. Despite our sinfulness, how do we often view ourselves according to the following verse? "Most men will proclaim each his own goodness" (Proverbs 20:6).

We view ourselves as "good" because we make the evaluation by comparing our behavior with that of other sinners. As a result, we do not end up looking too bad. But God's evaluation of us is based on His perfect standard. Therefore God's description of us as wicked, sinful enemies is very different from our description of ourselves as good people!

---

[3] Using the Ten Commandments to show us our sin is an effective method used by The Way of the Master.

8. What is the meaning of the word *death* in these verses?

   - "For the wages of sin is death" (Romans 6:23).
   - "Sin, when it is full-grown, brings forth death" (James 1:15b).

This word *death* speaks not only of physical death, but also of spiritual death and separation from God for all eternity. In other words, we *deserve* hell. This is a tragic situation in which we find ourselves, and without intervention from God, we would all end up in hell. Not only have we missed God's standard for heaven because of our sin, but we have actually *earned* eternal punishment.

But if God loves us, why can He not just overlook our sin? That is because...

God Is Just

God's justice is one of His least-understood attributes. Our English Bibles use the terms *justice* and *righteousness* interchangeably. Both terms speak of the fact that God is absolutely *right* in all He does.

9. How does this verse describe our incredible God?
   "He is the Rock, His work is perfect; for all His ways are justice, a God of truth and without injustice; righteous and upright is He" (Deuteronomy 32:4).

Because God is absolutely just, He *must* punish sin. For the sake of illustration, let's say you commit three relatively small sins a day (you would be doing *very* well!). But if God gives you seventy years on earth, you would meet your Maker with more than seventy thousand violations of His holy law on your record! To put that into perspective, would it be reasonable for you to stand before federal court with seventy thousand violations of the federal law on your record and expect to walk free? No! Then why would you expect a heavenly Judge, who is infinitely more just than a human judge, to overlook your violations against His law? That would render God an unjust judge. Simply put, God *must* punish sin. And that punishment is death and eternal separation from God.

Man's sin constitutes the bad news. Now for the good news…

Jesus Saves

So we have sinned, and according to the Bible, we deserve death and eternal separation from God in hell. But the story does not end there! It becomes absolutely and remarkably amazing!

10. According to the following verse, what does God require for the remission (forgiveness) of sins? "Without shedding of blood there is no remission" (Hebrews 9:22b).

Blood is a symbol of death. In Old Testament times, the people were required to make animal sacrifices. An innocent animal was put to death in the sinner's place. This was a picture of what the promised Messiah would one day do for the sins of mankind. Christ, the innocent, shed His blood and died for the guilty. He took the punishment for our sins so we could be forgiven.

It is as if you are standing before a judge. You have been found guilty of crimes that warrant your death. There is a resounding *bang* as the judge's gavel comes down and the judge announces the verdict–*"Guilty!"* What a contradiction it would be for that same judge to walk down from his place, remove his judge's robe and place it on you saying, "I will take your punishment for you. You may go free." *That is what Christ has done for us!* Jesus will one day judge our sins. He will find us guilty of crimes that warrant our death. But this just Judge can forgive our sins without punishing us because He has already taken the punishment that our sins require! He shed His innocent blood on the cross for our sins–the just died for the unjust!

11. What two words do the following verses use to describe Christ?

   • "For Christ also suffered once for sins, the just for the unjust, that He might bring us to God" (1 Peter 3:18).
   • "Greater love has no one than this, than to lay down one's life for his friends" (John 15:13).

Christ's death for us on the cross proves that God is *just* and that He is *love*! While His justice demands that sin be punished, His love caused Him to take our punishment on Himself! Absolutely amazing!

Christ made salvation possible, what, now, must *we* do?

Repent and Believe

Christ Himself taught that we must "repent and believe in the gospel" in order to gain eternal life (Mark 1:15). The word *repent* denotes an inward attitude of contrition or regret for past sins that leads us to forsake them. It is a change of *heart* that leads to a change in *behavior*. One who asks forgiveness for his wrongdoing only to immediately repeat the sin again proves that he was not truly sorry. His actions speak louder than his words. True heartfelt sorrow over having sinned against a holy God causes us to not only seek forgiveness from God but to hate our sin and turn from it. This kind of sorrow over sin and change of heart can come only as the Holy Spirit convicts us and changes us.

12. What does the following verse tell us godly sorrow ultimately leads to? "For godly sorrow produces repentance leading to salvation, not to be regretted; but the sorrow of the world produces death" (2 Corinthians 7:10).

Notice the two different sorrows in this verse. Godly sorrow is grieving over sin; worldly sorrow is grieving over the *consequences* of our sin. In other words, salvation *requires* repentance and repentance comes from a deep conviction and sorrow over our sins. Throughout the Bible God commands us to repent of our sins. In fact, God makes it very clear that salvation comes *only* to those who truly repent. Consider the following verses on repentance. Repentance is not an option!

- "I tell you, no; but unless you repent you will all likewise perish" (Luke 13:3).
- "[God] commands all men everywhere to repent, because He has appointed a day on which He will judge the world in righteousness" (Acts 17:30–31).

True repentance will change us from the inside out. The change in outward behavior is due to the change of heart. Consider the following:

8

13. How does Romans 6:17–18 describe a person before salvation? After salvation? "But God be thanked that though you were slaves of sin, yet you obeyed from the heart that form of doctrine to which you were delivered. And having been set free from sin, you became slaves of righteousness."

Notice that these verses clearly state that we are all slaves. Before salvation we are slaves to sin; we are in bondage to our sin nature with its selfish desires and passions. After salvation we are slaves of righteousness.

14. As slaves of righteousness, for whom should we live once we are saved? "He died for all, that those who live should live no longer for themselves, but for Him who died for them and rose again" (2 Corinthians 5:15).

15. What does the following verse say is the reason Christ died for us?
    "[Christ] gave Himself for us, that He might redeem us from every lawless deed and purify for Himself His own special people, zealous for good works" (Titus 2:14).

Christ did not die so that we could continue to wallow in the mire of our sin. No! He died to *redeem* us from that sinful condition, to purify us, and give us the desire to live lives that are pleasing to Him.

Many people say a prayer to "accept Christ as their Savior" but never turn from their sins in repentance. Their life after their "salvation" is much the same as it was before. Tragically, they will be among the group that Jesus describes in Matthew 7:21–23:

> "Not everyone who says to Me, 'Lord, Lord,' shall enter the kingdom of heaven, but he who does the will of My Father in heaven. Many will say to Me in that day, 'Lord, Lord, have we not prophesied in Your name, cast out demons in Your name, and done many wonders in Your name?' And then I will declare to them, 'I never knew you; depart from Me, you who practice lawlessness!'"

16. What do the people in this passage think is their eternal destiny?

17. What do they base their belief on?

18. Who does this passage say will go to heaven?

These people thought they were saved because of their good works, but they had never turned in repentance from their sins to do the "will of the Father." They had continued living life *their* way. On judgment day they will hear the tragic words, "I never knew you; depart from Me." There will be no greater tragedy.

So repentance is an inward attitude of remorse for sins that leads to a change in outward behavior. But repentance was only half of Christ's command in Mark 1:15. He also commanded us to "believe in the gospel." First Corinthians 15:3–4 defines what the word *gospel* means in the biblical sense: "Christ died for our sins according to the Scriptures, and that He was buried, and that He rose again the third day according to the Scriptures." The word *gospel* refers to Christ's death, burial, and resurrection on our behalf. To "believe the gospel" means that we believe we are sinners deserving of eternal punishment. But that God, in His goodness to us, sent His Son to suffer and die in our place so our sins could be forgiven by a just God. Christ's death on the cross is our *only* means of eternal life. We cannot earn heaven or ever deserve it based on our own good works.

19. According to Philippians 3:9, how do we become righteous in God's eyes? "And be found in [Christ], not having my own righteousness, which is from the law, but that which is through faith in Christ, the righteousness which is from God by faith."

In other words, no matter how hard we try to obey God's law, we will never attain the perfect righteousness that God requires. Perfect righteousness comes through faith in Christ and His death on the cross on our behalf. When we repent of our sins at salvation, not only does God forgive our sins, but according to Scripture, He actually gives us the righteousness of Christ in return. In other words, though Christ lived a perfectly righteous life (without sin), God credits that righteousness to our account as if we had never sinned! The prophet Isaiah states this marvelous truth by saying, "He has clothed me with the garments of salvation, He has covered me with the robe of righteousness" (Is. 61:10).

20. Consider the following verse. If we can get to heaven by trying to live good, moral, law–abiding lives, then what did Christ do? "If righteousness comes through the law, then Christ died in vain" (Galatians 2:21).

21. What did Jesus say is the *only* way to heaven? "Jesus said to him, 'I am the way, the truth, and the life. No one comes to the Father except through Me'" (John 14:6).

Salvation, then, does not come from saying a prayer or walking down an aisle. It comes from a *change of heart*. Having lived life *our* way, we repent of our sin and selfishness and trust in Jesus Christ *alone* to save us. That change of heart can be expressed to God through prayer:

> "God, I know you are holy but I am a sinner. Because of my sins, I deserve to be eternally separated from you. But because of your great love for me, you sent your Son, Jesus, to be punished in my place. I repent of my sins and desire from this day forward, with your help, to turn from living life my way to live a life pleasing to you. I would like for you to be both my Savior and my Lord. Thank you for giving me the gift of eternal life!"

"For God so loved the world that He gave His only begotten Son, that whoever believes in Him should not perish but have everlasting life."
John 3:16

2

Spiritual Growth

The following passage is a great summarization of what we discussed in chapter one:

> "For the grace of God that brings salvation has appeared to all men, teaching us that, denying ungodliness and worldly lusts, we should live soberly, righteously, and godly in the present age, looking for the blessed hope and glorious appearing of our great God and Savior Jesus Christ, who gave Himself for us, that He might redeem us from every lawless deed and purify for Himself His own special people, zealous for good works" (Titus 2:11–14).

1. What does this passage say "brings salvation" to us?

The word "grace" means unmerited favor. In other words, we do not deserve God's salvation. It is His underserved kindness to us.

2. What must we "deny"?

3. As Christians, how should we live once saved?

As citizens of the heavenly kingdom (Phil. 3:20) living in a sinful, fallen world, we must "deny" or repent of living a life of ungodliness and choose to live our lives pleasing to God. Therein lies the essence of the Christian life! A life totally transformed from serving self to serving the Savior! This transformation, which theologians call *sanctification*, does not happen overnight. While salvation is a point-in-time event, sanctification begins at salvation and is a process that lasts a lifetime. Sanctification is the process whereby the Holy Spirit uses God's Word (John 17:17), prayer (Phil. 4:6), worship (Ps. 95:6), Christian fellowship (Acts 2:42), witnessing (Matt. 28:19-20), self-discipline (Gal. 5:23), and a myriad of other things, to mature us spiritually and conform us to the image of Christ.

4. According to Romans 8:29, to what did God predestinate us?
   "For whom He foreknew, He also predestined to be conformed to the image of His Son…"

5. What happens to us as we "behold" the glory of Christ as He is revealed in God's Word? "But we all, with unveiled face, beholding as in a mirror the glory of the Lord, are being transformed into the same image from glory to glory, just as by the Spirit of the Lord" (2 Corinthians 3:18).

Just like a mirror reflects our image, the Bible reflects the image of Christ. The more we study Christ's image, the more like Him we become. This comes from the work of the Holy Spirit in the

Christian's life. The more like Christ we become, the more we can then reflect the glory of Christ to a sinful world. As such, Christ-likeness must be the priority of every believer. We are commanded to pursue Christ-likeness, holiness (Heb. 12:14), and godliness (1 Tim. 4:7). These are synonymous terms that speak of an inward devotion to God that is manifested in outward behavior. God does not want us to merely clean up our act but to be so devoted to Him that our behavior is radically changed from the pre-salvation person we once were.

6. The comparison of the pre-salvation person and the post-salvation person is clearly expressed in 2 Corinthians 5:17. According to this verse, what happens when we are saved? "Therefore, if anyone is in Christ, he is a new creation; old things have passed away; behold, all things have become new."

When we repent of the self-focused life to live the Savior-focused life, everything about us changes. We no longer say the things we used to say, go to the places we used to go, watch the things we used to watch, do the things we used to do. Life takes on an entirely different purpose. We are no longer consumed with our own pleasure but with God's pleasure. This transformation is a change that begins immediately at the time we are saved but continues to grow throughout life. This process of growing in godliness is not an easy process. Like most things of value, it takes time and effort.

Exercising Unto Godliness

7. What do these verses say godliness requires? "Exercise yourself toward godliness. For bodily exercise profits a little, but godliness is profitable for all things, having promise of the life that now is and of that which is to come" (1 Timothy 4:7–8).

8. How much of our life is affected (or profited) by being a godly person?

9. Godliness profits us not only in this life but what else?

The word *exercise* connotes hard work and self-discipline. One who wants to become a first-class football player will spend a great deal of time on the field exercising to the point of exhaustion. We are often willing to put a great deal of effort into some areas of our lives, whether it be sports, hobbies, or work, but we often expect our growth in godliness to happen with little effort on our part. It will not! The Apostle Paul says it requires hard work.

Paul assures us that the time and effort required to grow in godliness is absolutely worth the energy spent. In fact, he says that godliness will not only profit us in this life but also in the life to come. Now we are speaking of eternal consequences! The effort we put into most things will only profit us in the present life. But the godliness we achieve now, through the Holy Spirit's enabling, will profit us for all eternity. That puts growing in godliness in a league of its own!

10. What are we to give our attention to and meditate on according to 1 Timothy 4:13 and 15? "Till I come, give attention to reading, to exhortation, to doctrine... Meditate on these things; give yourself entirely to them, that your progress may be evident to all."

11. What did Paul mean by "give yourself entirely to them"?

12. What will be the result of putting such effort into knowing God's Word?

13. Is your spiritual growth evident to those around you?

The Hebrews Heroes

Hebrews 11, known as the "Faith Chapter," gives us some amazing accounts of Old Testament men and women who had a devotion for God that radically influenced the way they lived. As a result, God was able to use these heroes of the faith in remarkable ways. Their lives stand in stark contrast to the lives of those who do not take growing in godliness seriously. Let's look at a few of these heroes:

14. When God warned Noah of the worldwide flood that was to occur, what did Noah's deep faith in God cause him to do? (Note: This job took a hundred and twenty years of *hard* labor!) "By faith Noah, when warned about things not yet seen, in holy fear built an ark to save his family" (Hebrews 11:7, NIV).

15. God made many promises to Abraham that were to be fulfilled through Abraham's only son, Isaac (Gen. 17). Yet, God commanded Abraham to sacrifice Isaac on an altar (Gen. 22). What caused Abraham to offer up Isaac? (Note: This was only a test. God provided a lamb in place of Isaac.) "By faith Abraham, when God tested him, offered Isaac as a sacrifice... Abraham reasoned that God could even raise the dead" (Hebrews 11:17, 19, NIV).

16. Moses was raised as the adopted son of Pharaoh's daughter. As such, he had all the possessions and power he could want, yet he gave it all up to suffer as a slave with his Jewish people. What caused him to make this unbelievable sacrifice? "By faith Moses, when he had grown up, refused to be known as the son of Pharaoh's daughter. He chose to be mistreated along with the people of God rather than to enjoy the fleeting pleasures of sin. He regarded disgrace for the sake of Christ as of greater value than the treasures of Egypt, because he was looking ahead to his reward" (Hebrews 11:24–27, NIV).

The question we must ask is: *What caused these men (and the other men and women in Hebrews 11) to make such incredible sacrifices for God?* Would the average twenty-first century Christian be willing to spend a hundred and twenty years in hard labor to build an ark when he or she had never witnessed rain? Would an everyday, run-of-the-mill Christian have the faith in God to offer his only son on an altar at God's command? Would today's typical Christian relinquish a life of astounding luxury to become a slave for God's sake? No! So what causes the difference between the way we live as Christians and the way these Hebrews 11 heroes of the faith lived?

These heroic men and women had such a deep love and devotion for their God that they lived each day focused on *heavenly* realities rather than *earthly* ones. Their heavenly focus caused them to live extraordinary lives for the Lord. The behavior of these three men was not a result of personality, upbringing, or station in life, but, rather, a direct consequence of their devotion to God.

From Ordinary To Extraordinary

Consider the twelve disciples who were handpicked by Jesus for spreading the gospel to the whole known world. Instead of choosing men of high rank with religious training, Jesus chose twelve extremely ordinary men. Not one was known for his scholarship or public speaking ability.

17. How were the *leaders* of the twelve disciples described in Acts 4:13? "Now when they saw the boldness of Peter and John, and perceived that they were uneducated and untrained men, they marveled. And they realized that they had been with Jesus."

We can relate to these men because they were prone, like we are, to wrong attitudes (Matt. 20:20–28), lack of faith (Matt. 17:14–21), and utter failure (Mark 14:43–52). Yet, despite their faults and failures, Jesus invested approximately eighteen months of intensive training into these disciples. He taught them the Scriptures and how to live godly lives. He exhibited a life of truth, love, forgiveness and humility to them. Eleven of the twelve disciples emerged from this training time completely and totally transformed. With the help of the Holy Spirit, they turned the world upside-down with the gospel of Jesus Christ!

18. According to the preceding verse (Acts 4:13), what was the secret to the disciples' radical transformation from ordinary to extraordinary?

We, too, must *be with Jesus* if we are to be transformed from the ordinary to the extraordinary!

Dealing With Distractions

The story of Mary and Martha gives us insight as to what our priorities should be.

> "Now it happened as they went that [Jesus] entered a certain village; and a certain woman named Martha welcomed Him into her house. And she had a sister called Mary, who also sat at Jesus' feet and heard His word. But Martha was distracted with much serving, and she approached Him and said, 'Lord, do You not care that my sister has left me to serve alone? Therefore tell her to help me.' And Jesus answered and said to her, 'Martha, Martha, you are worried and troubled about many things. But one thing is needed, and Mary has chosen that good part, which will not be taken away from her'" (Luke 10:38–42).

19. What did Mary do while Jesus was in her home?

20. What did Martha do while Jesus was present?

21. Which woman did Jesus commend as doing the best thing? Why?

According to social etiquette in the first century, women did not socialize with men. They served men. For this reason, Martha believed strongly that she and Mary should be serving refreshments to Jesus and His companions while they were in the sisters' home.

Martha, irritated with Mary for not helping, voiced her complaint. Jesus' response is significant. Jesus was more pleased with the one who was sitting at His feet learning than the one who was allowing the busyness of life to distract her.

We, too, must spend time with Jesus if we are to be godly Christians fit for the Master's use. This will require training or "exercise." This requires being committed to reading God's Word, praying, attending church, and fellowshiping with other believers. This is God's plan for spiritual growth. There is no shortcut. As you commit one day at a time to being faithful in your spiritual exercises, God will give you the desire to grow and be faithful. But if you quit, your desire for God and His will for your life will also wane. You must be faithful!

Being faithful in these spiritual disciplines will take endurance. Endurance is greatly enhanced when goals are established to keep us on track. The Apostle Paul, using the Corinthian Games as a metaphor, stresses the importance of running the Christian race with a goal in mind, not aimlessly:

> "Do you not know that in a race all the runners run, but only one gets the prize? Run in such a way as to get the prize. Everyone who competes in the games goes into strict training. They do it to get a crown that will not last, but we do it to get a crown that will last forever. Therefore I do not run like someone running aimlessly; I do not fight like a boxer beating the air. No, I strike a blow to my body and make it my slave so that after I have preached to others, I myself will not be disqualified for the prize" (1 Corinthians 9:24–27).

Notice Paul's comparison between the life of an athlete and that of a Christian:

1). Those who run in a race run with the goal of receiving the prize. As Christians, we do not compete against each other but against the obstacles that hinder us spiritually.

2). Those who compete in a race go into "strict training." As Christians, we must go into strict training by reading God's Word, praying, attending church, etc. Again, "strict training" (another word for *exercise*) is not easy! It takes endurance and hard work.

3). Runners in an earthly race receive a prize that will not last. Christians receive a prize that will last for all eternity!

4). As Christians, we cannot run "aimlessly" or as one "beating the air." Many Christians remain spiritually immature because they wander aimlessly from day to day without the "strict training" that is required to grow spiritually. Like Martha, they are allowing the busyness of life to keep them from focusing on God's goal for them–the goal of Christ-likeness.

We will discuss setting goals more in-depth in the following chapters. For now, keep in mind that an athlete who practices consistently may not see improvement within a day or even a week. But he should be able to look back over a year's time and see a great deal of improvement. Growing in godliness is no different. Be faithful!

> **"O God, You are my God; early will I seek You;**
> **My soul thirsts for You; my flesh longs for You**
> **In a dry and thirsty land where there is no water."**
> **Psalm 63:1**

3

Bible Study

The Bible tells us that at the time of salvation we become the "children of God" (John 1:12). Just like babies born into this world in a physical sense must grow and mature physically, those born into God's family in a *spiritual* sense must grow and mature *spiritually.*

1. What do the following verses tell us to desire? "As newborn babes, desire the pure milk of the word, that you may grow thereby, if indeed you have tasted that the Lord is gracious" (1 Peter 2:2–3).

Almost from the moment of birth, a healthy infant will break out into loud, insistent demands for his mother's milk. Here, Peter is comparing the newborn infant's *strong* desire for milk to the newborn Christian's desire for the "milk" of God's Word. God designed the infant's first response to this world to correspond to his greatest need. Similarly, a newborn Christian ought to crave spiritual food from God's Word.

The Bible: The Christian's Instruction Book

Imagine what it would be like for someone from an ancient civilization, perhaps Alexander the Great, to be dropped in the middle of modern-day New York City. Though Alexander is known as one of the greatest military geniuses of all times, he has no knowledge of twenty-first century culture or technology. The poor man has never seen a car, bus, or airplane. He has no knowledge of traffic safety or streetlights. His survival skills are totally useless amidst the skyscrapers and busy streets. The crowds that speak a foreign language and behave in a totally alien way overwhelm him. Given the scenario, Alexander may not last long enough to explore the next block!

Though a humorous scenario to consider, it is not far from what we experience when we try to navigate this world without knowing the God who made it and sustains it. The world quickly becomes a painful cacophony of disruptions, disorder, and distress. We are not sure which way to go or what to do.

God has graciously given us His Word, the Bible, to instruct us on how to live the God-honoring life. In it He has set before us the truth about life and death, blessing and cursing (Deut. 30:19). He instructs us in the way we should go and the thing we should do (Jer. 42:3). He tells us of His love and forgiveness, His wrath and punishment (Ex. 34:6–7). In it He gives us clear instructions to follow for living the abundant life (John 10:10), the prosperous life (Ps. 1:2–3), the life of joy (John 15:11). He also gives us guidance for maneuvering through life's difficulties (Ps. 119:92). Simply put, the Bible has everything we need to know to live the Christian life.

2. In His instructions to us, how does God depict the Christian? "You therefore must endure hardship as a good soldier of Jesus Christ. No one engaged in warfare entangles himself with the

affairs of this life, that he may please him who enlisted him as a soldier" (2 Timothy 2:3–4).

Because we are soldiers fighting a war against Satan, the regular, daily intake of God's Word is absolutely crucial for the spiritual welfare of every Christian. Our adversary, the Devil, is called "the god of this world" (2 Cor. 4:4, KJV).

3. Of what are we warned in the following verse? "The whole world lies under the sway of the wicked one" (1 John 5:19).

The Devil is behind the world's philosophies, ideologies, and value systems. Because we live in a world ruled by the "wicked one," we are regularly bombarded with its corrupting influences and philosophies. Because God's perspective of life is the polar opposite of Satan's perspective, we must consistently saturate our minds with God's Word to understand and maintain the right perspective.

The Bible: A Source For Transformation

Consider the following verse:

> "Do not be conformed to this world, but be transformed by the renewing of your mind, that you may prove what is that good and acceptable and perfect will of God" (Romans 12:2).

4. What does Paul command us *not* to be?

5. To be *transformed* means to be *changed completely.* According to this verse, how do we make this change?

6. When our minds are *renewed,* what will we be better able understand?

Our minds are renewed as the Holy Spirit uses consistent Bible study to change our thinking. As our minds are renewed, our lives are transformed! There is simply no alternative way for growing spiritually than constantly saturating our mind with God's Word.

The Bible is not given to us primarily to be a source of *information* but as a resource for *transformation.*

7. According to 2 Corinthians 3:18, whose image are we being transformed into? "But we all, with unveiled face, beholding as in a mirror the glory of the Lord, are being transformed into the same image from glory to glory, just as by the Spirit of the Lord."

As we continually gaze at the glory of Jesus Christ revealed to us in Scripture, the Holy Spirit progressively transforms us into the image of Christ. The more we know Him, the more like Him we become! Remember, that is the very purpose for which God saved us–that we should be conformed to the glorious image of Christ (Rom. 8:29)!

The Bible: Its Transforming Benefits

The Bible has much to say about the transforming benefits of Bible study. Let's look at a few:

> "From childhood you have known the Holy Scriptures, which are able to make you wise for salvation through faith which is in Christ Jesus. All Scripture is given by inspiration of God, and is profitable for doctrine, for reproof, for correction, for instruction in righteousness, that the man of God may be complete, thoroughly equipped for every good work" (2 Timothy 3:15–17).

8. What does Paul tell Timothy that the Scriptures make us wise unto?

9. What else does Paul say the Scriptures are profitable for?

10. What is the goal of immersing ourselves into God's Word?

11. What two things does this verse say the Bible does for us? "So now, brethren, I commend you to God and to the word of His grace, which is able to build you up and give you an inheritance among all those who are sanctified" (Acts 20:32).

12. What are the benefits according to this verse? "For the LORD gives wisdom; from His mouth come knowledge and understanding" (Proverbs 2:6).

13. What does this verse say the "counsel" of God's Word does for us? "You will guide me with Your counsel, and afterward receive me to glory" (Psalm 73:24).

14. Of what profit is the Bible according to this verse? "Your word is a lamp to my feet and a light to my path" (Psalm 119:105).

15. Delighting in God's Word allows us to get through what? "Unless Your law had been my delight, I would then have perished in my affliction" (Psalm 119:92).

16. This verse mentions several reasons God gave us His Word. What are they? "For whatever things were written before were written for our learning, that we through the patience and comfort of the Scriptures might have hope" (Romans 15:4).

And we have only reviewed a fraction of the benefits we find in the Scriptures! It is no wonder that the more we know God's Word and recognize its value and worth, the more we love and desire it! The one who loves and desires God's Word will faithfully read it and, by the power of the Holy Spirit, be absolutely *transformed* by its message. It all starts with the Word of God!

17. Because the benefits of daily Bible intake are so vital to our spiritual success, what does God command us to do? "Study to shew thyself approved unto God, a workman that needeth not to be ashamed, rightly dividing the word of truth" (2 Timothy 2:15, KJV).

The Bible: The Christian's Passion

18. Developing a passion for God's Word is both essential and attainable. Read the following testimonies of faithful men who have gone before us. Circle the words in these verses that show how these men *felt* about God's Word.

- "I will delight myself in Your statutes; I will not forget Your word" (Psalm 119:16).
- "My soul breaks with longing For Your judgments at all times" (Psalm 119:20).
- "Oh, how I love Your law! It is my meditation all the day" (Psalm 119:97).
- "I rejoice at Your word As one who finds great treasure" (Psalm 119:162).
- "Your words were found, and I ate them, and Your word was to me the joy and rejoicing of my heart" (Jeremiah 15:16).
- "I have treasured the words of His mouth More than my necessary food" (Job 23:12).

These men had a passion for God's Word because they recognized that in it lay the formula, not only for eternal life, but also the successful life here on earth. When we recognize the extreme treasure we have in God's Word, we, too, will *delight* in it, *long* for it, *love* it, *rejoice* over it, and *treasure* it!

The Bible: A Resource For Success

19. What are God's plans for us according to Jeremiah 29:11? "'For I know the plans I have for you,' declares the LORD, 'plans to prosper you and not to harm you, plans to give you hope and a future'" (NIV).

Jeremiah tells us God wants us to prosper. Joshua tells us how:

> "This Book of the Law shall not depart from your mouth, but you shall meditate in it day and night, that you may observe to do according to all that is written in it. For then you will make your way prosperous, and then you will have good success" (Joshua 1:8).

20. What are we commanded to do day and night?

21. What are we commanded to do besides meditate on God's Law?

22. What is the final outcome of those who meditate on and obey God's Word?

We all want to prosper and be successful. Here is God's formula for success! This is a huge concept that we must take seriously! *True success comes from knowing and obeying God's Word.*

Jesus illustrated the incredible value of knowing and obeying God's Word by telling a story about a wise man and a foolish man:

> "Therefore whoever hears these sayings of Mine, and does them, I will liken him to a wise man who built his house on the rock: and the rain descended, the floods came, and the winds blew and beat on that house; and it did not fall, for it was founded on the rock. But everyone who hears these sayings of Mine, and does not do them, will be like a foolish man who built his house on the sand: and the rain descended, the floods came, and the winds blew and beat on that house; and it fell. And great was its fall" (Matthew 7:24–27).

Those who build their lives on the foundation of salvation and obedience to God's Word will find success in this life and the next. But those who allow the busyness of this life to keep them from reading and heeding God's Word will fall–and great will be their fall both in this life and in the judgment! How gracious God is to give us His instruction book so that we will know His will and build our lives on a firm foundation!

Suggestions For Bible Study

- **Set a goal.** Make regular, daily Bible study your goal. You may not always have the same amount of time every day to devote to studying God's Word but, nevertheless, try to spend some time *every* day.

- Start with prayer.
  - o Confess any sin in your life.
  - o Give God thanks for who He is and the blessings He has given you.
  - o Ask the Holy Spirit to illuminate your mind and aid you in understanding and applying the Bible's truths to your life.
- Choose a book of the Bible to study–the Gospel of John is a good book for new believers to start with. Read through the book you choose once for an overview. Try to read it in one sitting if possible. From then on, read each chapter one at a time slowly and carefully–multiple times is best. Examine the chapter for details.
- Have a notebook for recording verses that the Holy Spirit impresses upon you during your study. When the God of the universe uses His Word to speak to you, write it down! Don't forget it!
  - o Each day as you study, record the date in your notebook and the chapters being studied.
  - o Record verses that you find particularly convicting, encouraging, or interesting.
  - o Record at least one way in which you can apply what you read to your life. Meditate on this throughout the day.
- Your notebook will be of great value to you as it will allow you to review periodically the truths the Holy Spirit has impressed upon you. It also allows you to evaluate your faithfulness in daily Bible study. Your goal ought to be to have a journal entry for every day of the year. That is a lofty but attainable goal. By using a notebook you will be able to keep track of how you are doing.
- Seek to make daily Bible study a *priority*. Many people plan a full day and then try to stick a bit of Bible study in somewhere. If Bible study is a priority, we will plan our Bible study first.

"Your testimonies also are my delight and my counselors."
Psalm 119:24

4

Prayer

God is kind beyond measure and compassionate beyond words. He is "merciful and gracious, longsuffering, and abounding in goodness and truth, keeping mercy for thousands, forgiving iniquity and transgression and sin" (Ex. 34:6–7). The psalmist sums it up well, "The earth is full of the goodness of the LORD" (Ps. 33:5)!

God's goodness to us, as Christians, is beautifully described in Ephesians 1. It says that God has:

- Blessed us with every spiritual blessing in heavenly places (1:3)
- Chosen us in Him before the foundation of the world (1:4)
- Adopted us into His family (1:5)
- Made us accepted in the Beloved (1:6)
- Completely forgiven us (1:7)
- Made us to abound in God's wisdom and understanding (1:8–9)
- Obtained for us an inheritance (1:11)
- Sealed us with the Holy Spirit of promise (1:13)
- Purchased us (1:14)
- Made us to the praise of His glory (1:14)

It doesn't get any better than that!

Understanding God's goodness to us helps us understand the incredible value of prayer. The Bible often uses earthly fathers to represent God, our heavenly Father. Just as a loving and kind human father wants to give his children their requests, so our heavenly Father wants to please us–He who spared not His own Son for us! Consider the meaning of the following passage:

> "Ask, and it will be given to you; seek, and you will find; knock, and it will be opened to you. For everyone who asks receives, and he who seeks finds, and to him who knocks it will be opened. Or what man is there among you who, if his son asks for bread, will give him a stone? Or if he asks for a fish, will he give him a serpent? If you then, being evil, know how to give good gifts to your children, how much more will your Father who is in heaven give good things to those who ask Him?" (Matthew 7:7–11).

God wants to give us the desires of our heart–as long as they line up with His holy will for us. Let's look at what the Bible says about prayer.

1. According to James why do we often not have what we want or need? "You do not have because you do not ask" (James 4:2).

Consider the amazing truth of the following verse:

> "Yet the Lord longs to be gracious to you; therefore he will rise up to show you compassion. For the Lord

is a God of justice. Blessed are all who wait for him"
(Isaiah 30:18, NIV)!

2. What does God *long* to do?

3. What does the word *"grace"* mean (defined in Chapter 2)?

4. What must we do?

When problems come along, we often jump headlong into solving the problems the best we know how instead of taking the problems to God in prayer. James 4:2 clearly indicates a connection between asking and receiving, while Isaiah 30:18 reminds us that God is longing to help us with our difficulties. God *wants* to help us, but He often waits to be asked.

Prayer is a way for us to access the help available to us by an all-wise, all-powerful, and all-loving Father. Prayer is of incredible benefit to all who, convinced of its benefits, discipline themselves to use it. Yet, it is notoriously overlooked and seldom utilized by God's children. Henry Blackaby states, "The greatest untapped resource that I know of is the prayer of God's people."[4] Tragically, many believers, having read what the Bible teaches about prayer, walk away unchanged because they don't really believe what they have read.

---

[4]   Henry T. Blackaby and Claude V. King, *Experiencing God* (Nashville, TN: LifeWay Press, 1990), 143.

Reasons For Prayer

We are commanded to pray, not for God's sake, but for ours. Jesus tells us, "Your Father knows the things you have need of before you ask Him" (Matt. 6:8). In other words, God does not need for us to keep Him abreast of our problems and predicaments. He is omniscient (all-knowing). He is well aware of what we need even before we are! So why are we commanded to pray? The Bible's primary emphasis on the subject of prayer is on praying in faith.

Consider the message of these two verses: "Be anxious for nothing, but in everything by prayer and supplication, with thanksgiving, let your requests be made known to God; and the peace of God, which surpasses all understanding, will guard your hearts and minds through Christ Jesus" (Philippians 4:6–7).

5.   What does it mean to be anxious about something?

6.   What should accompany our prayers for God's help? Why?

7.   What does God give to those who pray instead of fret and worry?

Prayer is a vehicle through which we demonstrate to God that we trust Him as our good God, loving Father, powerful Provider, Great Physician, wise Counselor, and all the other attributes that make up His exceptional character. Prayer also keeps us ever mindful of our total dependence upon our Creator for even the bare necessities of life (Phil. 4:19). This dependence is beautifully illustrated by the psalmist who, in total dependence upon God, cried, "I will lift up my eyes to the hills, from whence comes my help? My help comes from the LORD, who made heaven and earth" (Ps. 121:1–2). The God who commanded the universe into existence by His word is certainly capable of caring for those He created!

Prayer brings God great pleasure when it is offered in faith and total dependence upon Him. In fact, the Bible tells us, "The prayer of the upright is His delight" (Prov. 15:8). We *delight* the heart of God when we spend time communing with Him in prayer!

Praying Effectively

The Scripture tells us, "The effective, fervent prayer of a righteous man avails much" (James 5:16). Let's examine some characteristics of an *effective* prayer.

8. First, what kind of prayer does the following verse say God will "hear"? "Now this is the confidence that we have in Him, that if we ask anything according to His will, He hears us" (1 John 5:14).

Knowing God's will about a matter requires knowing God's Word. Even then, the Bible does not reveal God's will concerning every situation that arises in our lives. In such cases, we should pray for a deeper understanding of what God's will is and for the grace to submit to that will.

9. Second, what kind of prayer does John 14:13 say Christ will honor? "And whatever you ask in My name, that I will do, that the Father may be glorified in the Son" (John 14:13).

In the ancient world, a person's name represented who he was. It represented his character. Praying "in Jesus' name" means praying in accordance with Christ's character and all that He is.

10. Third, according to the following verses, what does effective prayer require?

- "But your iniquities have separated you from your God; and your sins have hidden His face from you, so that He will not hear" (Isaiah 59:2).
- "He who covers his sins will not prosper, but whoever confesses and forsakes them will have mercy" (Proverbs 28:13).

God is a person, not a power. He is our compassionate and loving Father, not an abstract force. As such, sin breaks our fellowship with God so that He will not *hear* or attend to our prayers as He otherwise would. Therefore, we must deal with the sin by seeking forgiveness and thus restore our relationship before our prayers will be effective.

Learning To Pray

In one sense, prayer should be as second nature to the Christian as crying is to an infant. As the infant grows and advances intellectually, he begins to voice his needs more clearly and concisely. So it is with the Christian who, by way of discipline, has increased in the knowledge of God and His Word. He learns *how* to pray. So even though prayer is in one sense second nature, it is in another sense a learned discipline. That is why the disciples requested help from Jesus saying, "Lord, teach us to pray" (Luke 11:1).

Looking at what the Bible says about prayer, we find four important areas of prayer. We can remember them by the acronym ACTS.[5]

Adoration: As we reflect on God, His glory, His majesty, His goodness, we cannot help but praise Him for his excellent attributes!

11. What does Hebrews 13:15 exhort us to do? "Therefore by [Christ] let us continually offer the sacrifice of praise to God, that is, the fruit of our lips, giving thanks to His name."

God desires that we voice our praise and adoration to Him, not weekly or daily, but *continually*! This means living every moment mindful of the great God we serve. It means voicing our praise to Him on a regular basis. Consider the following example of adoration:

"Therefore David blessed the LORD before all the assembly; and David said: 'Blessed are You, LORD God of Israel, our Father, forever and ever. Yours, O LORD, is the greatness, the power and the glory, the victory and the majesty; for all that is in heaven and in earth is Yours; yours is the kingdom, O LORD, and You are exalted as head over all. Both riches and honor come from You, and You reign over all. In Your hand is power and might; in Your hand it is to make great and to give strength to all. Now therefore, our God, we thank You and praise Your glorious name'" (1 Chronicles 29:10–13).

Confession: As already noted, sin breaks our fellowship with God and hinders our prayers. As a result, we must continually seek forgiveness for our wrongdoing.

---

[5]   John MacArthur, *Fundamentals of the Faith* (Sun Valley, CA: Grace Community, 1993), 56.

12. What does God promise to do when we sincerely repent of sin? "If we confess our sins, He is faithful and just to forgive us our sins and to cleanse us from all unrighteousness" (1 John 1:9).

13. According to 1 John 1:9, is there any sin God will not forgive if it is confessed with a penitent heart?

Thanksgiving: The Bible is replete with commands to give thanks to God for *everything*. But it is only when we are convinced that God is all-powerful, all-wise *and all-good*, that we can truly give thanks during the good times and the bad. We must believe that even the trials we experience are given to us by a *good* God to perform His *good* work in our lives. That is why James, the brother of Jesus, tells us to count it all joy when we experience trials. After all, it is the trials in our lives that God uses to mature us spiritually and make us fit for His service (James 1:2–4).

14. What are we told to do in Ephesians 5:20? "Giving thanks always for all things to God the Father in the name of our Lord Jesus Christ."

15. What does the psalmist say we should "sacrifice"? "Oh, that men would give thanks to the LORD for His goodness, and for His wonderful works to the children of men! Let them sacrifice the sacrifices of thanksgiving, and declare His works with rejoicing" (Psalm 107:21–22).

Supplication: Scripture is packed with admonitions to be diligent in our prayers and supplications (specific requests). It tells us to:

- Pray without ceasing (1 Thess. 5:17)
- Continue earnestly in prayer, being vigilant in it (Col. 4:2)
- Continue steadfastly in prayer (Rom. 12:12)
- Praying always with all prayer and supplication in the Spirit (Eph. 6:18)

These admonitions are given repeatedly because prayer impacts the way God acts! The Bible tells us, "You do not have because you do not ask" (James 4:2). This verse clearly indicates that failure to go to God with our needs and requests often deprives us of what God would otherwise have given us. This truth is beautifully illustrated for us in the lives of King Hezekiah and King Asa.

16. What was the result of Hezekiah's prayer? "In those days Hezekiah was sick and near death. And Isaiah the prophet, the son of Amoz, went to him and said to him, 'Thus says the LORD: "Set your house in order, for you shall die and not live."' Then Hezekiah turned his face toward the wall, and prayed to the LORD, and said, 'Remember now, O LORD, I pray, how I have walked before You in truth and with a loyal heart, and have done what is good in Your sight.' And Hezekiah wept bitterly. And the word of the LORD came to Isaiah, saying, 'Go and tell Hezekiah, "Thus says the LORD, the God of David your father: 'I have heard your prayer, I have seen your tears; surely I will add to your days fifteen years.'"'" (Isaiah 38:1–5).

17. Upon whom did King Asa rely for healing? "And in the thirty-ninth year of his reign, Asa became diseased in his feet, and his malady was severe; yet in his disease he did not seek the LORD,

but the physicians. So Asa rested with his fathers; he died in the forty-first year of his reign" (2 Chronicles 16:12–13).

It was not a sin for King Asa to seek help from the physicians. The sin was in relying on them to do what only God can do. We are specifically told that King Asa did not seek God's help. God does not promise to heal us, but He does want us to put our confidence in Him, not in the doctors. Asa did not ask, and he did not receive.

Submitting to God's Will

God does not always choose to give us our request. There are a variety of reasons for this.

18. As we have already noted, when God does not give us our request, what does 1 John 5:14 imply might be the problem? "Now this is the confidence that we have in Him, that if we ask anything according to His will, He hears us."

19. What does James say might be the reason for not getting our request? "You ask and do not receive, because you ask amiss, that you may spend it on your pleasures" (James 4:3).

20. James also gives another reason for not getting our request. What is it? "But let him ask in faith, with no doubting, for he who doubts is like a wave of the sea driven and tossed by the wind. For let not that man suppose that he will receive anything from the Lord" (James 1:6–7).

There are also times God honors our request but not on our timetable; we have to wait. The Jews prayed for hundreds of years for God to send the promised Messiah but it wasn't until "the fullness of the time had come, God sent forth His Son" (Gal. 4:4).

We are encouraged to be persistent in our prayers (Luke 18:1–5). But when God does not give us our request, we must submit to His perfect will (James 4:7). God is not a puppet waiting to do our beck and call. In fact, we are told, "He does according to His will in the army of heaven and among the inhabitants of the earth" (Dan. 4:35). But of one thing we can always be sure, God is trustworthy and He is good–in all things, at all times, no matter the situation.

Prayer Journal

Set a goal. Make it your goal to meet with God in prayer every day. Remember, it must be a *priority*. The spiritual disciplines take discipline!

- Record praises and prayer requests in a journal or notebook (nothing is too big or too small to take before God). This will help you keep focused as you pray and will aid you in remembering your requests.
- As prayer requests are answered, mark the date that the request was answered by the request to remind you of God's goodness in hearing your prayer. These requests have now become items for thanksgiving!

"Call to Me, and I will answer you, and show you great and mighty things, which you do not know."
Jeremiah 33:3

5

Worship

The word *worship* means *worth-ship.* To worship God is to attribute to Him the proper worth. The more we know God and understand his glorious attributes, the more we can respond to Him with hearts of worship. Many vacation every year in the Smoky Mountains having never experienced the glorious Swiss Alps. Likewise, many Christians are content to know a little about God because they have not experienced the awe and wonder of knowing Him more fully. God becomes bigger to us as we know Him more deeply. As we know Him more deeply, we can worship Him more fully.

God reveals Himself to us primarily in three ways. According to the following verses, what are they?

1. "For since the creation of the world His invisible attributes are clearly seen, being understood by the things that are made, even His eternal power and Godhead, so that they are without excuse" (Romans 1:20).

2. "My son, if you receive my words, and treasure my commands within you, so that you incline your ear to wisdom, and apply

your heart to understanding… then you will understand the fear of the LORD, and find the knowledge of God" (Proverbs 2:1–2, 5).

3. "No one has ever seen God, but the one and only Son, who is himself God and is in closest relationship with the Father, has made him known" (John 1:18, NIV).

Because God reveals Himself to us through nature, the right response to a spectacular sunset or a magnificent mountain view is a heart of worship for our all-powerful Creator. As we seek the knowledge of God by reading His Word, our heart should soar in praise to our good and faithful God. As we see the heart of love and compassion of Jesus in Scripture, we bow our knees in humble adoration to the One who most clearly reveals the Father to us–for He is God (John 1:1).

The God We Are To Worship

Psalm 29:2 tells us, "Ascribe to the LORD the glory due his name; worship the LORD in the splendor of his holiness" (NIV). In order to give God the glory due Him, we must have an understanding of His "unsearchable" greatness (Ps.145:3). Listed below are verses that help us understand more fully the greatness of our God. After each verse, summarize what God has revealed about Himself.

4. "I will lift up my eyes to the hills from whence comes my help? My help comes from the LORD, who made heaven and earth" (Psalm 121:1–2).

5. "Great is our Lord, and mighty in power; His understanding is infinite" (Psalm 147:5).

6. "'Can anyone hide himself in secret places, so I shall not see him?' says the LORD; 'Do I not fill heaven and earth?' says the LORD" (Jeremiah 23:24).

7. "For You, Lord, are good, and ready to forgive, and abundant in mercy to all those who call upon You" (Psalm 86:5).

8. "The LORD, the LORD God, merciful and gracious, longsuffering, and abounding in goodness and truth, keeping mercy for thousands, forgiving iniquity and transgression and sin" (Exodus 34:6–7).

9. "He who does not love does not know God, for God is love" (1 John 4:8).

10. "He is the Rock, his works are perfect, and all his ways are just. A faithful God who does no wrong, upright and just is he" (Deuteronomy 32:4, NIV).

11. "The LORD has established His throne in heaven, and His kingdom rules over all" (Psalm 103:19).

12. "Because it is written, 'Be holy, for I am holy'" (1 Peter 1:16).

13. "For the wrath of God is revealed from heaven against all ungodliness and unrighteousness of men, who suppress the truth in unrighteousness" (Romans 1:18).

God's wrath is a righteous wrath focused specifically on sin. A God who did not hate sin would not be worthy of our worship. Christians, however, have no need to fear God's wrath. Although before salvation we "were by nature children of wrath," we now have a Savior "who delivers us from the wrath to come" (Eph. 2:3, 1 Thess. 1:10). In other words, Jesus Christ bore God's wrath toward our sins for us! As a result, "There is therefore now no condemnation to those who are in Christ Jesus" (Rom. 8:1). God Himself suffered in the person of Jesus Christ to deliver us from the wrath we deserve!

Worship Acceptable To God

Worship must be done according to God's standard in order to be pleasing to Him. Let's look at what the Bible says about God-honoring worship.

14. What does Jesus say constitutes true worship in John 4:23–24?
    "But the hour is coming, and now is, when the true worshipers

will worship the Father in spirit and truth; for the Father is seeking such to worship Him. God is Spirit, and those who worship Him must worship in spirit and truth" (John 4:23–24).

To worship in "spirit" is to worship with our heads *and* hearts engaged in an active preoccupation with the greatness of God. Attending a Sunday worship service with our minds and emotions in neutral does not qualify as worship. We may sing, pray, and take notes on the sermon, but if our inner man is not preoccupied with God then we are not worshiping but merely attending. On the other hand, a trip to the botanical gardens may be a time of exuberant worship as we praise the great Gardener for His handiwork. Remember, "The LORD searches all hearts and understands all the intent of the thoughts" (1 Chronicles 28:9). True worship comes from the heart.

To worship in "truth" means we must worship God as He is revealed in Scripture. God is a God of love *and* wrath, mercy *and* justice. To stress only one side of His attributes, such as the love and mercy, without wrath and justice, is not worshiping the God of Scripture.

Biblical Worship

The word *worship* is used two different ways in Scripture. In the broad sense, it denotes a way of life. In a more narrow sense, it denotes the specific activity of praising God for His excellence.

Worship As a Way of Life

15. According to the following verse, what does worship as a way of life entail? "Therefore, I urge you, brothers and sisters, in view of God's mercy, to offer your bodies as a living sacrifice, holy and

pleasing to God—this is your true and proper worship" (Romans 12:1, NIV).

16. How does King Hezekiah describe his life of worship? "Remember, LORD, how I have walked before you faithfully and with wholehearted devotion and have done what is good in your eyes" (2 Kings 20:3).

17. Psalm 100 is a well-known Psalm calling us to worship God in a variety of different ways. As you read the Psalm, number the seven different commands we are given in it (each starts with a different verb).

Psalm 100

"Make a joyful shout to the LORD, all you lands!
Serve the LORD with gladness;
Come before His presence with singing.
Know that the LORD, He is God;
It is He who has made us, and not we ourselves;
We are His people and the sheep of His pasture.
Enter into His gates with thanksgiving,
And into His courts with praise.
Be thankful to Him, and bless His name.
For the LORD is good;
His mercy is everlasting,
And His truth endures to all generations."

It is obvious that there are many different ways to worship God. This Psalm speaks of voicing our praise to God through shouting and singing. It also speaks of our obligation to serve God with hearts of gladness. It expresses our obligation to know God, which entails spending time in His Word. We are told to "enter His gates with thanksgiving and His courts with praise." This refers to worshiping God in a public worship service. And, to top it off, we are to be thankful to Him and bless His name. Everything we do with the intent to praise and glorify God is a form of worship. It is a way we show God how worthy He is of our devotion.

Worshiping as a way of life entails dedicating our mind, emotions, and will to God. It encompasses our attitudes and actions. It requires having a mindset that seeks to glorify God in everything we do throughout the day. It is *living* righteously.

18. What does Paul say is the result of a life lived in true worship? "For we are to God the fragrance of Christ among those who are being saved and among those who are perishing" (2 Corinthians 2:15).

Just as the smell of baking brownies will permeate the house, we are to allow God's glory to permeate the world around us by the way we live. Paul states that God, through us, "diffuses the fragrance of His knowledge in every place" (2 Cor. 2:14). What a great description of how we influence others when we live our lives in continual worship to God! Bear in mind, this way-of-life worship takes great effort and constant focus. But it enables those around us to see God *in us*.

Worship as a Specific Activity

In the narrow sense, worship is the act of praising God for who He is. We must be careful, here, to remember that true worship must be done with the right "spirit." We may give thanks for a meal out of habit rather than true gratefulness and miss the standard for true worship. Likewise, a song of praise sung with a disengaged heart falls short of genuine worship. Tragically, much of our "worship" is done in a passive frame of mind rather than out of an active desire to gratify and glorify our great God.

19. Consider the following verses carefully. What was the offense for which Jesus rebuked the Pharisees? "Hypocrites! Well did Isaiah prophesy about you, saying: 'These people draw near to Me with their mouth, and honor Me with their lips, but their heart is far from Me. And in vain they worship Me'" (Matthew 15:7–9).

20. In contrast, how did King David worship God? "I will praise You, O Lord my God, with all my heart, and I will glorify Your name forevermore" (Psalm 86:12).

Private Worship Versus Public Worship

While private worship is very important, our worship of God should not be limited to individual, private worship. In fact, God has set aside one day each week in which we are commanded to meet with other believers and worship God corporately in a group setting.

21. What were the Jews commanded in the Old Testament to do in regard to the Sabbath? "Remember the Sabbath day, to keep

it holy. Six days you shall labor and do all your work, but the seventh day is the Sabbath of the Lord your God. In it you shall do no work… therefore the Lord blessed the Sabbath day and hallowed it" (Exodus 20:8–11).

22. According to the following verses, what are we commanded not to forsake? Why? "And let us consider one another in order to stir up love and good works, not forsaking the assembling of ourselves together, as is the manner of some, but exhorting one another." (Hebrews 10:24–25).

23. According to Ephesians 4:11–12, for what reason did God give gifted men to the church? "And He Himself gave some to be apostles, some prophets, some evangelists, and some pastors and teachers, for the equipping of the saints for the work of ministry, for the edifying of the body of Christ."

24. This verse lists another way church members can profit from godly leaders within the church. What is it? "Remember those who rule over you, who have spoken the word of God to you, whose faith follow, considering the outcome of their conduct" (Hebrews 13:7).

Not only do we profit from the ministry of church leaders, the Bible commands individual believers within a local church to minister to one another in various ways. Some refer to these as the "one another" passages. Believers in a local church are told to pray for one another (James 5:16); be kind to one another (Eph. 5:21); serve one another (Gal. 5:13); comfort one another (1 Thess. 4:18); forgive one another (Col. 3:13); admonish one another (Rom. 15:14); teach one another (Col. 3:16); encourage one another (Heb. 3:13); love one another (1 Peter 1:22); edify one another (1 Thess. 5:11); bear one another's burdens (Gal. 6:2); submit to one another (Eph. 5:21); show hospitality to one another (1 Peter 4:9); prefer one another (Rom. 12:10); and to restore one another (Gal. 6:1). These various ministries are an essential part of the church as a whole and *absolutely vital for the spiritual well-being of each individual member within the church.* Just like a rope of many strands is far stronger than each strand individually, God has designed Christians within the local church to strengthen each other.

We all go through difficult times in life. When we do, we have God's people within our local church to come alongside us, to pray for us, encourage us, comfort us, and love us. They will serve us when we need to be served and admonish us when we need to be admonished. We, in turn, are to do the same for others when they go through hard times. In other words, God works through His people to help us through hard times. But what if we are not a part of a local church and do not have a network of Christian friends? In many ways, we have separated ourselves from the support that God intends for us to have.

Set a goal. Make it your goal to be in church every Lord's Day. The benefits of consistent, weekly church attendance cannot be overstated. God has chosen to use His people in the local church to serve and minister to one another in a myriad of different ways. When we do not honor Him with faithful church attendance, we cut ourselves off from the many blessings that could be ours.

"Praise the Lord! I will praise the Lord with my whole heart, in the assembly of the upright and in the congregation."
Psalm 111:1

6

Obedience

Throughout the Bible a saving relationship with Jesus Christ is inseparably linked to holy living. The Apostle Paul, once a blasphemer, persecutor, and violent aggressor against God's people, was radically transformed into a passionate man of God (1 Tim. 1:12–13). He describes his radical transformation in Galatians 2:20 where he says, "I have been crucified with Christ; it is no longer I who live, but Christ lives in me; and the life which I now live in the flesh I live by faith in the Son of God, who loved me and gave Himself for me." Paul is saying that the man he used to be, his old sinful man, was crucified. It is dead. In its place is the new man in which Christ dwells. The life he now lives is actually the life Christ is living through him. That explains the radical difference between his pre-salvation behavior and his post-salvation behavior. And that is the testimony of every *true* believer! Before we are saved we are ruled by our selfish, sinful nature, "the old self." When we repent of living life our way at salvation and put Christ on the throne, His Spirit comes to dwell within us. Using His Word, church, prayer, other believers, and a myriad of other things, Christ changes us from the inside out. Let's look at this process a little more closely.

The Old Self

1. What is meant by the "old things" which are "passed away" in the following verse? "Therefore, if anyone is in Christ, he is a new creation; old things have passed away; behold, all things have become new" (2 Corinthians 5:17).

When our old, sinful man is crucified, with it goes our old value system, our old goals and desires, our sinful perspectives. These are replaced by new values, goals, desires and perspectives. As we continue to grow spiritually, we think and act more and more in a way that pleases our Lord.

2. Consider carefully Galatians 6:14. What does Paul mean by "the world"? "But God forbid that I should boast except in the cross of our Lord Jesus Christ, by whom the world has been crucified to me, and I to the world."

Paul is not speaking of the physical world since he was still living in it. Nor is he speaking of humanity as we are told to love and serve others, not cut ourselves off from them. Paul is speaking, rather, of the invisible world system ruled by Satan, the "god of this world" (2 Cor. 4:4). Apart from Christ, a person is ruled by his own fleshly desires that are fed by the philosophies and values of the evil world system dominated by Satan. This kind of life is characterized by self-gratification and can lead to gross immorality and reckless abandon of what we know to be right. This is what Paul says every *true* Christian is dead to. We can still be influenced by the world's value system at times (which we must fight against), but we are no longer dominated and enslaved to it.

3. Galatians 5:24 also speaks of being crucified. What does this passage say the Christian is dead to? "And those who are Christ's have crucified the flesh with its passions and desires."

Before salvation the goals and desires we have for our lives are radically different than God's goals and desires for our lives. Romans 2:8 refers to the unsaved as "those who are self-seeking." When we repented of the sin of living the self-focused life to living the Savior-focused life, we committed to living by a whole new set of values and priorities.

4. Reflect upon the truth of James 4:4. What does God call those who live by the world's value system? "Do you not know that friendship with the world is enmity with God? Whoever therefore wants to be a friend of the world makes himself an enemy of God" (James 4:4).

This is a truth to be taken very seriously. Those who make little to no effort to break away from their worldly, sinful habits have great reason to doubt their salvation. John tells us, "If anyone loves the world, the love of the Father is not in him" (1 John 2:15).

The sins that dominated us before salvation may still tempt us after our salvation. We may even struggle intensely with them, but they should no longer rule us to the point that we are characterized by them or practice them habitually like we once did. For instance, the person once characterized by being argumentative before salvation will probably struggle with the same sin after salvation. The difference is that person is now struggling to overcome it through the power of the Holy Spirit. The desire to be Christ-like is now more important than the desire to always be right. We will still sin, but our life is no longer dominated by those sins which once ruled us.

The New Self

In Ephesians 4:21–24, Paul gives us an insightful comparison between the "old self" and the "new self." When reading these verses, keep in mind that this passage begins with the past tense verbs "were taught." In other words, Paul previously taught the Ephesian Christians about the necessity of putting off the "old self" and putting on the "new self" as this is a requirement for salvation. In this passage, Paul is merely reminding the Ephesian Christians of what they have already done.

Paul writes to the saints in Ephesus: "Assuming that you have heard about [Christ] and were taught in him, as the truth is in Jesus, (22) to put off your old self, which belongs to your former manner of life and is corrupt through deceitful desires, (23) and to be renewed in the spirit of your minds, (24) and to put on the new self, created after the likeness of God in true righteousness and holiness" (Ephesians 4:21–24, ESV).

5. According to Ephesians 4:21–24, what was our former way of life corrupted by? (22)

6. What makes the desires of the old self "deceitful"?

7. At salvation what was made new? (23)

8. As Christians, whom are we saved to be like? (24)

9. As Christians, what should our behavior be characterized by? (24)

10. How does Romans 6:4 describe our "walk" or behavior once we are saved? "Therefore we were buried with Him through baptism into death, that just as Christ was raised from the dead by the glory of the Father, even so we also should walk in newness of life."

Christ died *for* sin; we died *to* sin. Christ was raised back to physical life; we are raised to a *new life*–a life in Christ. This is what believer's baptism symbolizes. Being lowered into the water symbolizes our commitment (at salvation) to die to our old life of sin. Being raised out of the water symbolizes our commitment to live our life pleasing to Christ. Baptism is an *outward* testimony to an *inward* reality.

The Apostle Paul's use of analogies to explain spiritual truths is very helpful. In his letter to the Ephesians we see that Paul used the "old self/new self" analogy to explain the difference between what a person is like before he is saved and what that person is like after he is saved. In his letter to the Christians in Rome, Paul used the analogy of slavery to explain this concept.

Slaves

God's Word tells us clearly that we are all slaves. We are either slaves to sin or slaves to righteousness. There is no in-between group. We are either enslaved by our sinful nature and behave in accordance with our sinful desires and passions, or we are enslaved to God and His righteous standard for our life. In other words, some serve sin, the others serve the Savior.

Read Romans 6:17–22 slowly and thoughtfully:

> "But thanks be to God that, though you used to be slaves to sin, you have come to obey from your heart the pattern of teaching that has now claimed your allegiance. (18) You have been set free from sin and have become slaves to righteousness. (19)... Just as you used to offer yourselves as slaves to impurity and to ever-increasing wickedness, so now offer yourselves as slaves to righteousness leading to holiness. (20) When you were slaves to sin, you were free from the control of righteousness. (21) What benefit did you reap at that time from the things you are now ashamed of? Those things result in death! (22) But now that you have been set free from sin and have become slaves of God, the benefit you reap leads to holiness, and the result is eternal life" (Romans 17–22, NIV).

11. What is Paul referring to by "the pattern of teaching that has now claimed [our] allegiance"? (17)

12. Though we were previously enslaved to sin, those who have put their faith in Christ and repented of their sins are now enslaved to what? (18)

13. The end result of those who are slaves to sin is "death." This does not refer to physical death since all men die physically. What does "death" in this verse refer to? (21)

14. What does slavery to righteousness lead to in this life? What is its end result? (22)

15. Tragically, many claim to be Christians but their behavior clearly shows they are still enslaved by their sinful desires and passions. What does the following verse say their lives prove? "They profess to know God, but in works they deny Him, being abominable, disobedient, and disqualified for every good work" (Titus 1:16).

16. What does Titus 2:14 say was Christ's purpose in dying for us? "Who gave Himself for us, that He might redeem us from every lawless deed and purify for Himself His own special people, zealous for good works."

Remember, Christ died not only to save us from the *punishment* of sin (hell), but also from the *power* of sin. At salvation, when we truly repent of living life our way and put Christ on the throne, He breaks our bondage to sin, purifies us, and makes us fit for His good work.

Obedience–Proof Of Salvation

John's purpose for writing the book of 1 John is so that we can know for sure that we have eternal life (1 John 5:13). Read the following verses carefully:

> "Now by this we know that we know Him, if we keep His commandments. (4) He who says, 'I know Him,' and does not keep His commandments, is a liar, and the truth is not in him. (5) But whoever keeps His word, truly the love of God is perfected in him. By this we know that we are in Him. (6) He who says he abides in Him ought himself also to walk just as He walked" (1 John 2:3–6).

17. According to the above passage, what does John say proves that we are truly saved?

18. How does John describe the person who says he knows God but does not obey His commands?

19. What does John mean by walking "just as He (Jesus) walked"?

This passage describes two types of people. On the one hand are those who profess to know God but disobey His commands. John calls these people "liars." On the other hand are those who, out of love for God, keep His commands. John says these are truly God's children. Obedience to God proves we belong to Him.

Consider what John says one chapter later concerning obedience:

> "Little children, let no one deceive you. He who practices righteousness is righteous, just as He is righteous. (8) He who sins is of the devil, for the devil has sinned from the beginning. For this purpose the Son of God was manifested, that He might destroy the works of the devil. (10) In this the children of God and the children of the devil are manifest: Whoever does not practice righteousness is not of God" (1 John 3:7–8, 10).

It appears from this passage that there were many in the church to which John was writing who claimed to be Christians and "know God" but they lived in constant disobedience to His commands. John said they were deceivers. They claimed to be something they were not. Like them, the proof of our salvation is in how we live.

20. What does John mean by "he who practices righteousness"?

21. For what purpose did Jesus leave His home in heaven and manifest himself to us in human form? (8)

In this passage we are told that Christ was manifested to destroy the works of the devil. As Christians turn from their sins to live holy, obedient lives, the works of Satan are slowly being destroyed. They are not totally destroyed, but someday they will be. What a grand day that will be!

22. The following passage contains a huge truth for every believer. What is it? "You are of God, little children, and have overcome them, because He who is in you is greater than he who is in the world" (1 John 4:4).

In other words, Satan is not on equal ground with God. Satan is an angel who chose to rebel his Creator. Hence, he was thrown out of heaven along with others like him. Satan's power is limited. God's power is not. Presently God is allowing Satan to be the "ruler of this world" (John 12:31), but his time is limited. Ultimately, he will be thrown into the "lake of fire" where he will trouble us no more (Rev 20:10). God rules!

Set a goal. Make it your goal to walk in obedience to God's Word no matter what your emotions are telling you to do. Psalm 86:11 tells us, "Teach me Your way, O LORD; I will walk in Your truth; Unite my heart to fear Your name." Walking by truth means emotions no longer rule our decision-making!

"For this is the love of God, that we keep His commandments. And His commandments are not burdensome."
1 John 5:3

7

Serving

The Bible relates a fascinating story about a prophet named Elijah. We are told that, although Elijah was a very ordinary person just like you and me, God used him in amazing ways to accomplish His will (James 5:17–18). During the time of Elijah, the nation of Israel had fallen into such spiritual decline that most Israelites had taken up the worship of false gods. God instructed Elijah to gather the Israelites together—including the eight hundred and fifty false prophets. They were to erect two altars, one for the false god Baal, the other for the one true God. The God who provided fire from heaven to light the altar would prove to be the true God. Though the Baal worshipers cried loudly from morning until evening and cut themselves with knives, there was no response from Baal. When it was Elijah's turn, he prayed to God with a quiet, calm voice. The fire that God sent was so hot it consumed not only the sacrifice but also the wood and the stones on which the sacrifice lay. When the people of Israel saw it, "They fell on their faces; and they said, 'The LORD, He is God! The LORD, He is God'" (1 Kings 18:1–40)!

God gave Elijah instructions; Elijah obeyed. As a result, everyone in attendance clearly saw the power of the one true God. Just as God had specific jobs for which He called Elijah, God has specific jobs for each Christian. Let's look at what the Bible has to say about serving our great King.

Service Required

1. What four commands were the people of God given? "And now, Israel, what doth the LORD thy God require of thee, but to fear the LORD thy God, to walk in all his ways, and to love him, and to serve the LORD thy God with all thy heart and with all thy soul" (Deuteronomy 10:12, KJV).

2. What role (or "form") did Christ take upon Himself when He became a man? "But made himself of no reputation, and took upon him the form of a servant, and was made in the likeness of men" (Philippians 2:7).

3. According to Christ, what does becoming "great" require? "Whoever desires to become great among you shall be your servant. And whoever of you desires to be first shall be slave of all. For even the Son of Man did not come to be served, but to serve, and to give His life a ransom for many" (Mark 10:43–45).

4. According to the preceding verses, how did Christ serve us?

5. Serving God encompasses a wide range of activities. Some teach Sunday school classes, work in the church nursery, help maintain the church facilities, or prepare meals for the sick. In the following passage, Jesus served the disciples. What reason did He give them for His service to them? "[Jesus] rose from supper and laid aside His garments, took a towel and girded Himself. After that, He poured water into a basin and began to wash the disciples' feet, and to wipe them with the towel with which He was girded. So when He had washed their feet… He said to them… 'If I then, your Lord and Teacher, have washed your feet, you also ought to wash one another's feet. For I have given you an example, that you should do as I have done to you'" (John 13:4–5, 12–15).

In first century Palestine, open-toed sandals were commonly worn. The dusty roads made frequent washing of feet necessary. It was common courtesy upon entering a residence for a servant to wash the guest's feet. This foot-washing chore was reserved for the lowest servant. In washing the disciples feet, Christ modeled for us the humility and selfless service God desires of us. Ultimately, Christ humbled Himself and hung on a cross for those He came to save. There is nothing we should not be willing to do for Him!

6. Christians are clearly commanded in Titus 3:14 to serve God by serving others in a variety of different ways. How are Christians who are not serving described? "And let our people also learn to maintain good works, to meet urgent needs, that they may not be unfruitful."

7. What will Christians do in heaven for all eternity? "And there shall be no more curse: but the throne of God and of the Lamb shall be in it; and his servants shall serve him" (Revelation 22:3).

It is clear from the Scriptures that every Christian is called–and commanded–to serve his Savior. One pastor correctly stated, "Saving faith is a serving faith." Donald Whitney writes, "Serving God is not a job for the casually interested. It's costly service. He asks for your life. He asks for service to Him to become a priority, not a pastime."[6]

But this service must be done with the right motivation. Many Christians busy themselves doing good things to be seen of men or to fulfill a perceived duty. Works done for the wrong motivation do not please God. A religious leader once asked Jesus what the greatest and most important commandment was. Christ responded by saying, "You shall love the LORD your God with all your heart, with all your soul, and with all your mind. This is the first and great commandment" (Matthew 22:37–38).

8. Given the truth of Matthew 22:37–38, what should motivate our service to God?

For a husband to present flowers to his wife out of a sense of duty rather than love would be offensive. So it is with our service to God. It must be motivated by love. God loved us enough to send His Son to die for us. We should certainly love Him enough to give our lives in service to Him. Paul put this into perspective for us in Romans 12:1

---

6   Donald S. Whitney, *Spiritual Disciplines for the Christian Life* (Colorado Springs: NavPress, 1991), 116.

where he tells us that we should offer ourselves to God as a "living sacrifice" for this is our "reasonable service."

Service Empowered

9. What does Christ say we can accomplish for His kingdom by ourselves with no divine help from Him? "I am the vine, you are the branches. He who abides in Me, and I in him, bears much fruit; for without Me you can do nothing" (John 15:5).

10. What does Philippians 4:13 say we can accomplish with Christ's divine help? "I can do all things through Christ which strengthens me."

11. According to the following passage, God has not "called" (or saved) many of what kinds of people? "For you see your calling, brethren, that not many wise according to the flesh, not many mighty, not many noble, are called. But God has chosen the foolish things of the world to put to shame the wise, and God has chosen the weak things of the world to put to shame the things which are mighty... That no flesh should glory in His presence... As it is written, 'He who glories, let him glory in the LORD'" (1 Corinthians 1:26–27, 29, 31).

12. Why does God not choose to save many of these kinds of people?

13. Who gets the glory when the "foolish" and the "weak" do great things for God through His strength?

God deliberately calls the foolish and the weak into His service because it is through them He gets the greatest glory. The truth of this passage is amazing! God generally chooses to use the ordinary, not the extraordinary, to serve Him–people like you and me. God chose Abraham, who struggled with lack of faith and deception, to be the father of the Jewish race. He chose to save the pagan harlot Rahab and used her to help the Israelites take the city of Jericho. God chose Paul, a persecutor and murderer of God's people, to become the greatest missionary of all times. He chose the modern day Dwight L. Moody, a poorly educated shoe salesman, to preach the gospel to the unsaved. This ordinary, run-of-the-mill salesman became one of the greatest evangelists of modern times. God used him to bring thousands of souls across England and America into His kingdom. Henry Varley once said, "The world has yet to see what God can do with and for and through and in a man who is fully and wholly consecrated to Him."[7] We can do *all* things through Christ who gives us strength!

14. Not only does God give us the strength to serve Him, He also equips us with the spiritual gifts and abilities necessary to accomplish what He has called us to. According to the following passage, what does the Holy Spirit distribute to each Christian? "There are different kinds of gifts, but the same Spirit distributes them. There are different kinds of service, but the same Lord. There are different kinds of working, but in all of them and in everyone it is the same God at work." (1 Corinthians 12:4–6, NIV).

---

[7]   Henry T. Blackaby and Claude V. King, *Experiencing God* (Nashville: Lifeway Press, 1990), 24.

15. Does each Christian receive the same gift?

16. Who uses the gifts to accomplish His work through us?

Later in the same chapter, Paul compares the members of the local church to the members of a physical body. Each part of our body has a different job to do (whether it be the eye, kidney, or elbow, etc). Similarly, individual members of the church are given different spiritual gifts to accomplish different jobs within the church. If the eyes lose their ability to see, the whole body is greatly impacted. So it is with the church when individual members do not do the job God has called and equipped them to do. The whole church is impacted. The job may not get done at all, or others, who are gifted in other areas, must take up the slack and try to do their job and the jobs of members who are not serving.

17. According to Philippians 2:13, what two things does God work in us to accomplish? "For it is God who works in you both to will and to do for His good pleasure."

This verse tells us that God equips us to serve Him by giving us both the *desire* and the *ability* to serve Him. A church member with an interest and ability in gardening but no knowledge of electronics will most likely be called to help maintain the church grounds, not run the sound system. Similarly, an accountant with no experience with children would more likely be called to work with the church finances, not run the children's programs.

18. What does God give us to make us "abound" in the job He has called us to do? "And God is able to make all grace abound to you, so that having all sufficiency in all things at all times, you may abound in every good work" (2 Corinthians 9:8, ESV).

19. According to the following verse, who was working in and through Paul? "To this end I also labor, striving according to His working which works in me mightily" (Colossians 1:29).

Serving For The Glory Of God

Henry Blackaby writes, "The kind of assignments God gives in the Bible are always God-sized. They are always beyond what people can do, because He wants to demonstrate His nature, His strength, His provision, and His kindness to His people and to a watching world. That is the only way the world will come to know him."[8] The story of the Exodus clearly illustrates this. God warned Moses as the Israelites were leaving Egypt that He would harden Pharaoh's heart so that Pharaoh and his army would pursue the Israelites. God said He was going to do this so that He "would gain honor over Pharaoh and over all his army, that the Egyptians may know that I am the LORD" (Ex. 14:4). The Egyptian army pursued the Israelites, and God made a way of escape for them by parting the Red Sea.

God continued to work on the Israelite's behalf so that by the time they were preparing to enter the Promised Land (40 years later), the harlot Rahab from the pagan city of Jericho told the Israelite spies, "I know that the LORD has given you the land, that the terror of you has

---

[8]   Ibid., 116.

fallen on us, and that all the inhabitants of the land are fainthearted because of you. For we have heard how the LORD dried up the water of the Red Sea for you when you came out of Egypt, and what you did to the two kings of the Amorites who were on the other side of the Jordan, Sihon and Og, whom you utterly destroyed. And as soon as we heard these things, our hearts melted; neither did there remain any more courage in anyone because of you, for the LORD your God, He is God in heaven above and on earth beneath" (Joshua 2:9–11).

20. To whom did Rahab give the glory for drying up the Red Sea?

21. Although the Israelites fought and defeated those living in the land of Canaan, to whom did Rahab give credit?

22. What did seeing the mighty hand of God at work cause these idolatrous people to realize?

God gained glory for himself among a pagan, idolatrous people because He used plain, ordinary, flawed people to accomplish what only He could do.

Service Rewarded

God's Word is abounding with promises of reward for those who faithfully serve Him. In fact, it is amazing the number of times God repeats the promise of reward. We do not deserve rewards for serving the One who purchased us with His own blood, we owe it to Him

(Luke 17:10). Yet, once again, He graciously gives us what we do not deserve.

23. What two types of treasures are there, and which one are we commanded to store up? "Do not lay up for yourselves treasures on earth, where moth and rust destroy and where thieves break in and steal; but lay up for yourselves treasures in heaven, where neither moth nor rust destroys and where thieves do not break in and steal. For where your treasure is, there your heart will be also" (Matthew 6:19–21).

24. So important is the subject of rewards that God reminds us of it in His closing remarks to the New Testament. Obviously, He intends for us to take the subject seriously! On what does Jesus say the Christian's rewards are based? "And behold, I am coming quickly, and My reward is with Me, to give to every one according to his work" (Revelation 22:12).

Set a goal. Make it your goal to serve Christ in some capacity. Every Christian is called to serve Christ in some capacity. It is not only our duty, but it is our privilege. What we do for God will be rewarded far above what our service deserves. Our reward is not based on our success but on our faithfulness. The outcome of our service is in God's hands. We are only responsible for being faithful.

"Therefore, my beloved brethren, be steadfast, immovable, always abounding in the work of the Lord, knowing that your labor is not in vain in the Lord." 1 Corinthians 15:58

8

Loving As God Loves

In an attempt to express to the people of Israel God's unfathomable greatness, Moses described God to them as "the great God, mighty and awesome" (Deut. 10:17). Although this description is true, it does not come close to adequately describing God's "unsearchable" greatness (Ps. 145:3). To help us better understand His immense and infinite greatness, God often uses figurative language throughout the Bible to reveal Himself to us in terms we can understand. In the book of Isaiah He declares,

> "'To whom will you compare me?
> Or who is my equal?' says the Holy One.
> 'Lift up your eyes and look to the heavens: Who created all these?
> He who brings out the starry host one by one
> and calls forth each of them by name.
> Because of his great power and mighty strength,
> not one of them is missing'" (Isaiah 40:25–26, NIV).

Think about what God has revealed about Himself in these two verses. It is now estimated that the total star count is an unfathomable 300 sextillion! That is a three followed by twenty-three zeros. To put that into perspective, scientists estimate that there are ten times as many stars in the sky as there are grains of sand on all of Earth's beaches and deserts! God knows every intricate detail about each star–its temperature, its size, the gases it contains. After all, He created each one and hung it into place. He calls *each* star by name and sustains *each* one within its proper orbit.

But not only does God call each of the 300 sextillion stars by name, He goes on to say in the same chapter that "with the breadth of his hand [God] marked off the heavens" (Is. 40:12). The breadth of the hand (a common measurement in Isaiah's time) went from the tip of the thumb to the tip of the little finger. But how can one measure something as expansive as the heavens with the breadth of his hand? This is God's way of describing His limitlessness. He is totally beyond us.

Using the heavens to help us comprehend his greatness, God then describes humans in relation to Himself...

"[God] sits enthroned above the circle of the earth,
and its people are like grasshoppers" (Isaiah 40:22, NIV).

In other words, God is so great and man so insignificant, there is an incomprehensible chasm that divides the two. The psalmist totally understands the wonder of this when he cries:

"When I look at your heavens, the work of your fingers,
the moon and the stars, which you have set in place,
what is man that you are mindful of him,
and the son of man that you care for him?"
(Psalm 8:3–4, ESV)

That should be the question intriguing every person on this planet. *Why is the great and awesome God of such majesty and power "mindful" of such feeble and flawed earthlings such as us?* We may never understand on this side of eternity why a God of such magnificence would care for insignificant "grasshoppers" the way He does. But the wonder of it should impact our daily lives. What we *can* understand and *must* understand is the depth to which that great and awesome God is "mindful" of us and "cares" for us.

God's Love For Us

1. In 1 John 4:16, God gives us one of the best and most simple descriptions of Himself. What is it? "God is love, and he who abides in love abides in God, and God in him."

Notice that God does not describe Himself as "loving." We can all be loving at times. God says He *is* love. He is the essence of love. Therefore all that He does is out of His love for us. No exceptions.

2. How does Paul describe Christ's love for us? "That you, being rooted and grounded in love, may be able to comprehend with all the saints what is the width and length and depth and height–to know the love of Christ which passes knowledge" (Ephesians 3:17–19).

3. How does the prophet Jeremiah describe God's love? "Yes, I have loved you with an everlasting love; therefore with lovingkindness I have drawn you" (Jeremiah 31:1).

According to the preceding verses, the great God of the universe loves us with an inconceivably immense love that will never end. But what exactly is love? Is it an emotion? An act of the will?

Definition of Love

The Greek language in which the New Testament was written had several different words for our one English word *love*. There was a different word for romantic love, friendly love, the love of family members toward one another, etc. There was also a specific word for perfect love or God's love. It is *agape* love. This love is a selfless, giving love. Wayne Grudem writes, "God's love means that God eternally gives of himself to others."[9]

Consider the implications of God's *agape* love for us:

> "But God demonstrates His own love toward us, in that while we were still sinners, Christ died for us. (9) Much more then, having now been justified by His blood, we shall be saved from wrath through Him. (10) For if when we were enemies we were reconciled to God through the death of His Son, much more, having been reconciled, we shall be saved by His life" (Romans 5:8–10).

4. How did God "demonstrate" His love for us? Is God's love an active or passive love? (8)

---

9   Wayne Grudem, *Systematic Theology* (Grand Rapids: Zondervan, 1994), 198.

5. Because of our sin, what did we deserve instead of God's love? (9)

6. Where did we stand in our relationship to God when He gave His Son to die for us? (10)

What we are willing to pay for something is often a good indication of how much we value the object. The most expensive painting ever bought was a painting by Paul Cezanne entitled "The Card Players." It was bought in 2011 for a whopping $250 million! Let's look at what God was willing to pay for us...

7. We are told in 1 Corinthians 6:20 that we were "bought with a price." What was the price God paid for us? "Knowing that you were not redeemed with corruptible things, like silver or gold... but with the precious blood of Christ" (1 Peter 1:18–19).

God gave His Son–His *only* Son. When Christ came to live among us, He left the unbelievable splendor of heaven to be born in a filthy barn that no doubt smelled of animal feces. His parents were poor peasants from the lower-class area of Galilee. From youth, Jesus would have been expected to work hard to help support his poverty-stricken family. As an adult, Jesus selflessly gave of Himself to the point of exhaustion–healing the lame, blind, deaf, and speaking the words of God. Ultimately, He was hung on a cross by the very people He had come to save–the very people who had witnessed His miracles and heard His loving words of salvation. This is what the great and awesome God willingly paid in His love for us! This proves the *depth* of His love. It is a love that *passes knowledge* (Eph. 3:19).

Although perfect love involves emotions, it also involves much more. It involves the selfless act of the will. God loved us and gave Himself for us when we were His enemies (Col. 1:21). So why does God love us so selflessly? It is because He is a perfect God who exemplifies perfect love. His love for us has nothing to do with us. *God loves us despite who we are because of who He is!*

8. Consider the meaning of Isaiah 49:15–16. What does it mean that Christ has inscribed us on the palm of His hands? "Can a woman forget her nursing child, and not have compassion on the son of her womb? Surely they may forget, yet I will not forget you. See, I have inscribed you on the palms of My hands."

Given the truth of God's amazing love for us, let's consider what our response should be…

Loving God As He Loves Us

As Jesus was preaching to the crowds one day, a religious leader and expert in the Law of Moses came to Him to "test" Him. He asked Jesus a very important question: "'Teacher, which is the great commandment in the law?' (37) Jesus said to him, 'You shall love the Lord your God with all your heart, with all your soul, and with all your mind. (38) This is the first and great commandment. (39) And the second is like it: You shall love your neighbor as yourself. (40) On these two commandments hang all the Law and the Prophets'" (Matthew 22:36–40).

9. What did Jesus mean by His response, "You shall love the Lord your God with all your heart, with all your soul, and with all your mind"? (37)

10. What does "love your neighbor as yourself" look like in practical terms? (39)

11. What did Jesus mean by saying, "On these two commandments hang all the Law and the Prophets"? (40)

To love God with our whole heart, soul, and mind means to love Him with every part of our being, holding back *nothing*. God's love for us can be measured by what He was willing to give for us–His Son. Our love for God can likewise be measured by what we are willing to give to God. Remember, *agape* love is a sacrificial, giving love. And God wants our everything. He does not want our tithe without our time, or our Sundays without our Mondays. God's whole moral law can be divided into these two categories–loving God and loving our neighbor.

12. What is the meaning of the following verse? "Therefore, whether you eat or drink or whatever you do, do all to the glory of God" (1 Corinthians 10:31).

The word *glory* in this verse speaks of honoring or pleasing God. Paul is saying that even activities as mundane and routine as eating and drinking are to be done in a way that pleases God. In other words, God's honor and pleasure are to be our life's focus and commitment. When we love God with all of our being, we will sacrificially choose God's pleasure above our own.

13. What does God say is the secret to life, instead of death, and blessing, instead of cursing? "See, I have set before you today life and good, death and evil, in that I command you today to love the LORD your God, to walk in His ways, and to keep His commandments, His statutes, and His judgments... I have set before you life and death, blessing and cursing; therefore choose life" (Deuteronomy 30:15–16, 19).

What does Moses mean when he speaks of *life* and *death* in this passage? Paul, in Romans 10, refers back to this appeal of Moses. Paul equates the *life* spoken of here to eternal life, and the *death* to eternal death. In other words, God is warning us that our love for God, evidenced by our obedience to Him, will determine our eternal destiny. This love, of course, comes from believing what the Bible says about God and His relationship to humanity. He is righteous and loving. We are sinful and undeserving of Him. So God, at great expense to Himself, sent His Son to bridge the gap between the Righteous and the unrighteous. Christ took the curse we deserve, so that we can have the eternal life and blessing that we do not deserve. *That* is love!

Loving Others As We Love Ourselves

In answering the Pharisee's question concerning the greatest commandment, Christ also gave us the second greatest command– "love your neighbor as yourself" (Matt. 22:36–40). This is indeed a tall order! In the following parable, Jesus not only tells us who our neighbor is, but what loving him as we do ourselves looks like.

"But he, wanting to justify himself, said to Jesus, 'And who is my neighbor?' Then Jesus answered and said: 'A certain man went down from Jerusalem to Jericho, and fell among thieves, who stripped him of his clothing, wounded him, and departed, leaving him half dead. Now by chance a certain priest came down that road. And when he saw him, he passed by on the other side. Likewise a Levite, when he arrived at the place, came and looked, and passed by on the other side. But a certain Samaritan, as he journeyed, came where he was. And when he saw him, he had compassion. So he went to him and bandaged his wounds, pouring on oil and wine; and he set him on his own animal, brought him to an inn, and took care of him. On the next day, when he departed, he took out two denarii, gave them to the innkeeper, and said to him, "Take care of him; and whatever more you spend, when I come again, I will repay you." So which of these three do you think was neighbor to him who fell among the thieves?' And he said, 'He who showed mercy on him.' Then Jesus said to him, 'Go and do likewise'" (Luke 10:29–37).

14. According to Jesus, who is our neighbor?

15. In practical terms, what does it mean to love our neighbor as ourselves?

It is helpful to note that the priest and the Levite who passed by the beaten Jewish man without stopping to help were religious leaders.

Of all people, they would have been expected to display mercy and kindness to their fellow Jew. The Samaritan man, on the other hand, was from a group of people who were *despised* by the Jews. The Samaritans were a mixed people. They were Jews who had inter-married with Gentiles. As such, they were considered by the Jewish community to be pagans–pagans not worthy of treading the same planet! Not only did this kind Samaritan stop to help his "enemy," but his journey was delayed and he paid two days worth of wages for the man's hotel bill! *This* is the kind of love we are to have toward those around us–the same giving love that Christ has toward us.

First Corinthians 13 is known as "The Love Chapter." In it we find the most comprehensive biblical description of *agape* love. Read each phrase from this chapter slowly and thoughtfully. Evaluate how you are doing at displaying each facet of *agape* love.

> "Love suffers long and is kind; love does not envy;
> love does not parade itself, is not puffed up; does not
> behave rudely, does not seek its own, is not provoked,
> thinks no evil; does not rejoice in iniquity, but rejoices
> in the truth; bears all things, believes all things,
> hopes all things, endures all things. Love never fails"
> (1 Corinthians 13:4–8).

Set a goal. Make it your goal to love God with your whole heart, soul, and mind and your neighbor as yourself. Remember, *agape* love is a selfless, giving love. God is our supreme example. *God loves us despite who we are because of who He is!* He expects for us to do the same.

**"By this all will know that you are My disciples, if you
Have love for one another." John 13:35**

Printed in the United States
By Bookmasters